ABOUT THIS BOY

LEON ROLLE LOCKSMITH FROM RUDIMENTAL
+ DEREK OWUSU

WALKER
BOOKS

First published 2022 by Walker Books Ltd
87 Vauxhall Walk, London SE11 5HJ

2 4 6 8 10 9 7 5 3 1

Calligraphy by Kevin Rooi
Front cover photograph © 2022 Cesar Antonis
Portrait (of Leon Rolle) by Double or Nothing Productions

This book has been typeset in Sabon, Futura,
Clarendon and Sensory Overload

Printed and bound by CPI Group (UK) Ltd, Croydon CR0 4YY

British Library Cataloguing in Publication Data:
a catalogue record for this book
is available from the British Library

ISBN 978-1-5295-0062-2

www.walker.co.uk

For my eleven-year-old son, Leonyedus.
This book is my personal gift to you in the hope that it will have a positive impact on your journey through life.
Love you for ever, best friends, promise! – L.R.

For Berthy – D.O.

CONTENTS

HI FROM LEON

Hi, I'm Leon Rolle, but you might know me better as Locksmith from Rudimental. Before I was a global rock star, I was a kid from Hackney in East London. I loved doing the same things you do: hanging out with my friends, watching TV, playing video games, kicking a football and, of course, making music.

I loved football and music growing up. They were my passions, and they both gave me so much. Football was my first love. When I was a young kid, it was the most important thing in my life. I thought about it all day and I dreamed about it all night. I wanted to be a professional footballer, and I played for Arsenal's youth team until I was sixteen. But in the end life took me down a different path. And that's OK, because that's what life's all about.

I love being in Rudimental and I love my band mates. Music has always been the backdrop to everything I've done. I like the way it can lift you up and make you understand your emotions. Music is also a place for escapism and expression. You can get lost in making music and it can make you feel like you're creating a whole new world, rather than staying in the one you're in.

Music has meant I've done some amazing stuff in my life, like touring the world and scoring five UK Number One hits. And now I'm here, writing this book to tell you what I wish I'd known growing up. I love that I'm in a position to help kids, like you, to be the best version of yourself. And none of that would have happened if my life had been different.

A lot of this book was inspired by my son. I was pretty young when he was born, and I felt a wave of responsibility to be the best man I could possibly be, for him. I didn't grow up with a father, so I didn't know what that meant. I wasn't scared at the thought of becoming a dad, though. I was excited as this was another challenge for me.

I wanted to have a kid early in life because I wanted to give a kid all the things I didn't have when I was growing up. I'm not talking about material things. I'm talking about life stuff. I just wanted to be there for my kid. Mostly, though, I wanted my kid to know that it's not about whether things go well or badly in life, but how you cope with them.

It wasn't easy for me growing up and I made mistakes. But I don't regret what happened, because it made me who I am today, and mistakes are just a part of life.

No matter who you are, what you look like or where you come from, with the right attitude, you have the power to be great. I hope this book will inspire you to embrace life's successes and its failures. They are just a part of growing up and becoming you.

Thanks for reading!

Leon Rolle
Locksmith from Rudimental

YOUR EMOTIONS DON'T CONTROL YOU

It was July 2015 and I'd just stepped out onto the stage at Wembley Stadium with my band mates to hear everyone screaming the lyrics to one of our songs. The lights were really bright. The crowd looked like 90,000 shadows moving around with the music. But if I squinted, I could see some faces.

I was sweating. My shirt was stuck to my body, and there were so many more songs to go. When I left the stage, it would look like I'd jumped into a swimming pool with my clothes on. My band mates were around me, and I was jumping up and down with the mic in my hand. It was an amazing feeling. I loved it.

Out of the thousands of people who come to my concerts, I always look like I'm having the most fun. When I'm on stage, I feel in control of everything. If I stop the music, people will stop moving. If I shout into the microphone and ask the crowd to do something, they will do it. It's the best feeling in the world. But it's a performance. I'm putting on a show: it feels like I could step out of my body and watch myself.

When I was a young boy, it was the same. My emotions have always been so strong, but because I was always confident in front of people, no one had a clue I was hiding this turbulence inside. So, I felt alone.

I grew up in an area called Hackney, in East London. It was one of those loud places. Every time you walked down the street, people would be talking like we all wanted to hear their conversation. There were no mobile phones back then so everyone spoke face to face, and the streets always looked busy with people.

I lived with my mum and my two sisters. (My dad had lots of kids so I had more brothers and sisters too, but they didn't live with us. And my dad wasn't in the picture either.) Our house was as busy inside as the streets were outside. This meant I always had a mini audience around me, and I played to it.

We all have that cousin or sibling who we secretly think is a show-off. That was probably me. You could put me in front of any crowd of people, and I would feel confident and in control while I was performing. The word performing is important because it means that you're not really being you. That's how you could describe me when I'm in front of people or a crowd.

I've never had an issue standing up in front of people. When I was younger, I wasn't performing music as such, but I was always happy to get up and dance around and get the party started. But it was like someone else took me over, like I was two people in one. When I was in front of a group of people, it was as though there was a smaller version of myself hiding inside me. Probably curled into a ball. Probably sad and lonely. And angry. No one would know about him except me. Often no one looked for the real me behind the performance, and that made me feel angry and alone, which had a big impact on my behaviour.

The first time my emotions exploded was in Year Three. You don't really do much in Year Three and the teachers are so happy there isn't much to be upset by. Except if you have a Jamal in your year. Jamal was always moving about and fiddling with stuff. He couldn't keep his hands off things. And that included me. He didn't bully me, but he got on my nerves on purpose.

He loved to do things to get me upset.

If he walked behind me, he would try and step on the back of one of my shoes so it came off.

Annoying.

He would poke me while I was trying to listen to our teacher read us a story.

Annoying.

Or he would flick my ear when I was working.

So annoying.

I would walk to the toilets and cry. That's how I dealt with it. Sitting on a toilet seat with my hands covering my eyes. I thought I was upset at how he was treating me. But I think they were hot tears of anger that I couldn't control what was happening to me and my emotional reaction to it.

There was one week when Jamal had been doing a lot to me. More than usual. It was like nonstop. And, finally, I decided it was enough.

I thought about what I was going to do to Jamal all weekend. I even daydreamed about hiding a pair of scissors in my sock and then if he came near me, I would pull them out. He would be scared and leave me alone. But I could never do that in real life. It was stupid and wrong. Instead, I decided that I was going to fight him if he came up to me in class.

I was so angry when I got to school on Monday. I had been angry all through Saturday and Sunday, and by school, I was ready to explode with it. I knew by getting ready to fight Jamal I was preparing to do something wrong, but I didn't care. I wanted to be left alone, and I couldn't see any other way to make that happen.

For some reason, that day Jamal didn't bother me as much as usual. Maybe he could sense I was fed up. Then, finally, he walked up to me, but before he said anything or tried to touch me, I grabbed him. I threw him on the floor and I was pulling at his clothes and dragging him around. I was screaming too. I must have looked crazy. I'm a bit embarrassed to be telling you this now, to be honest, but at the time I just felt so mad, and I didn't know how to handle it.

The teachers ran over and pulled me off him. I was crying again, like I often did, but this time I knew exactly why. I was angry. Angry with Jamal but angrier with myself for not being able to control my reactions to what he was doing.

And that was the beginning of many angry outbursts.

My behaviour at school got bad. I would go from being confident and happy to trying to trash our classroom. And it was always small things that set me off. Like someone taking my pencil case. And then I would pick up chairs and throw them all over the room. Other kids were sent out so that I could be controlled. But that wasn't easy. I must have seemed like the Incredible Hulk or something. The teachers were confused. Even the ones that understood me. They would try and talk me out of my anger and help me get control of my emotions. But it only lasted until the next time someone upset me.

And it wasn't just happening at school but on the football pitch too.

You probably know me for my music, but football has been part of my life since I can remember. It was my first passion, my first love. You could say I was born dribbling, and I would play football any chance I got. I loved it. Playing at the weekend was the highlight of my week, until everything started getting out of control. It was a confrontation with a ref that made me realize that my emotional outbursts needed to be sorted out.

I can't remember who we were playing, but I remember we were losing. The ref kept on making bad calls and it was getting on my nerves. Someone would jump into a tackle with two feet and he wouldn't even touch his whistle. But if I got the ball with fair foot action, it felt like he was blowing in my ear. *Beep beep beep*. It was like he was trying to annoy me on purpose. I could feel the anger burning inside me and still he kept blowing his whistle – *beep beep beep* – until I wanted to scream or throw something.

Finally, I couldn't take it any more.

I ran over to him and started shouting.

"You don't know what you're doing. You're an idiot!" I was this little kid telling this grown man he was useless at his job.

He blew his whistle again to order me off the pitch. *Beep beep beep.*

And I lost it. I got so angry; it all happened in a second. It felt like I wasn't in control of anything. I started kicking him over and over. Can you believe that? And I was screaming at him and I couldn't stop. "You're an idiot. I hate you!" I kept saying.

The ref didn't fight back. He was just trying to get me off him, but the more he tried to stop me, the harder and faster I kicked. I was still fighting him when some adults watching the game came to help. I was kicking so much that they had to pin me to the floor to try and calm me down, and that made me madder.

"Why are you holding me down?" I shouted.

"Because you tried to fight the referee!" one of my team-mates said. "You can't do that!"

There were all these shocked faces staring at me, all these people I played football with every week. People I liked and cared about, and it was too much. I was ashamed of my behaviour and my temper, and I knew I couldn't keep doing this. I had to understand why I was behaving like this and to try and change. I wasn't just letting my team down; I was letting myself down.

But where was my anger coming from and why could I not control my emotions?

After thinking about it as hard as I could, I decided it wasn't my fault. It was because I didn't have a dad. With one of my parents missing, I was like half a person. How could I control my emotions if I wasn't a complete person?

For a while that made things better, because I felt I wasn't responsible for my behaviour. If I got upset and cried, it was because of him. If I threw chairs and kicked people, it was because of him. If I said a swear word or shouted, I blamed him.

Then one day, after another outburst at school, my mum sat me down and talked to me. "Leon," she said, "you have to stop this."

I could feel myself getting upset. I was like a can of Coke being shaken up. "It's not my fault," I said. "It's because of Dad. If he was here, I'd be fine."

She thought about this for a moment and then said, "If your dad isn't here, how can he teach you to do bad things and be angry?"

I didn't know the answer to that, so I crossed my arms and pretended not to listen. In reality, I was listening really hard. This was the first time I'd felt properly heard in a long time.

"Do you blame your dad for all the good things about you as well as the bad?" she asked.

"No," I said immediately. Dad wasn't about. He didn't deserve credit for anything I did. And suddenly I understood. *I* needed to take responsibility for my actions. I couldn't blame a shadow or an invisible person. No one was in control of me except me. And I could control me. I just had to learn how to do it.

And that was the beginning of a real change in me.

It took time. Nothing happens overnight.

But after that, when I got upset or angry, I would replay what had happened in my head and I would ask myself what I could have done differently. Then the next time I would try to stop and think before I let my emotions take over.

I also worked on learning to open up and express myself. I wish I'd talked to people earlier, especially my mum. I was so mad at my dad that I didn't realize my mum had been there for me all along. My dad not being in my life hurt me, but I wish I could have seen that having one parent who cared and listened was more than enough. Then maybe I wouldn't have tried to fight that referee. And maybe I wouldn't have thrown chairs or tried to beat up Jamal.

But I had the key now. The first key on my journey to becoming Locksmith.

I want to share a secret with you: I still get mad and cry sometimes. I still let my emotions get the better of me now and then. And there's nothing wrong with that. That's normal.

But now I ask myself why I am crying, or why I am mad. What emotion am I feeling? Am I responsible for it, and if not, how do I take back control in this situation and not feel attacked by the feelings making me react like this?

And you can do that too. It will help you to understand yourself better and that will make new or difficult situations easier to deal with. Talking to people who love and care about you will help too.

Remember, change takes time, so don't expect anything to happen overnight, but slowly you can look at how you've reacted to things and you can decide how you want to be different in the future.

LIVE YOUR PASSION

Is there something you love more than anything else in the world? Something that you would do all the time if you could? For me, growing up, that was football. I felt like I could not breathe unless I was around a football. I loved it so much, I even slept with the ball.

So, when I was asked a few years ago to give a talk to the Under-10s at the Arsenal Academy, I was excited. As I looked at all their young faces, I saw myself. Not in their facial features, but in how eager they were. They couldn't wait to kick some more ball. Just like me when I was their age (and me now, to be honest). It was like their bodies were shaking because they couldn't control how excited they were for football.

I knew exactly how they felt!

I told them a story someone had told me when I was younger. It starts with a young boy asking his wise old grandfather how he can tell if he genuinely loves something or is passionate about it.

His grandfather thinks for a moment and then says, "Meet me at the beach tomorrow and I will show you."

The boy wakes up the next morning and dashes to the beach, excited to learn something new about himself. When he gets there, his grandfather is standing in the sea, and he tells the boy to come and join him. When the boy walks into the water, the grandfather says, "Duck under the water and stay there for as long as you can."

The boy is confused, but he trusts his grandfather, so he does as he says and puts his head below the waves. He stays there until his lungs are bursting, and then, gasping for air, he surfaces.

"How did that feel?" his grandfather asks.

"Not good."

"Why not?"

"Because I wanted to breathe really badly."

His grandfather smiles then and says, "When you want something as badly as you just wanted to breathe, then you know you are passionate about it."

This is how I felt about football when I was eight. When I woke up in the morning, the first thing I did was take my football from under my covers, put it on the floor and walk with it to the bathroom. I brushed my teeth passing the ball from one foot to the other. I washed staring at the ball waiting for me on the bathroom floor. I ate breakfast with the ball under my foot. Then I said bye to my mum and ran to school with the ball still at my feet.

The morning routine was drilled into my head. I always left home at about 7.50 a.m. School started at nine, but the caretaker opened the gates at eight and I'd get there early to play football. I was usually the first one there. I loved being on the ball. It felt like gliding through the air. I could breathe like I never had before.

I wanted to be the best and I trained hard. Experts say that to be very good at something you need to spend at least 10,000 hours doing it. That sounds like a long time. But when you're passionate about something, 10,000 hours isn't enough time. It feels so good to do what you love that time doesn't mean anything. I am a prime example of getting your 10,000 hours in; I've always been that way. It was the same when I was learning to mix records when I was older. I would be at my decks for six hours a day, trying to beat match two tunes together.

But back then, before I started Djing, all I wanted to do was play football. When I was in class I used to stare at the clock, willing time to go faster because I could not wait to get out and kick a ball. And when I was playing, I never knew how much time had passed because I was enjoying myself so much. I didn't care if my team won or lost; I would still be happy at the end of a match because every game I played was making me a better player.

My dream was to do 100 kick-ups in a row. The first time I tried I only did around twenty. But I was determined. So, I focused my passion and I broke down how I was going to achieve 100. Every day I practised for an hour. I started by doing one kick-up at a time.

One kick-up then stop.

One kick-up then stop.

Then I moved on to two.

Two kick-ups then stop.

Two kick-ups then stop.

After a few hours, I was the king of doing two kick-ups. And I continued like this, one kick-up at a time, until I reached 100 in a row. It took a while, but on the day I did it I was so happy and proud.

It was obvious to anyone who knew me, or saw me play, that football was my life. And it made me disciplined. Me and my friends would play every day for an hour before lessons, an hour at lunchtime and then after school for as long as we could. The caretaker would ask us every night: "How long will you boys be making a noise tonight, then?"

We played in something called a cage. It was just like a football pitch but without the grass or turf. It was just concrete with a metal cage all around the pitch. The caretaker never locked up because he knew we would just climb over the fence, and that was dangerous. He was a nice guy. He cared more about our safety than finishing work early. We couldn't have cared less about our safety when playing football. And we always played till late.

I remember one night in particular. I must have been about nine or ten, and we were having a great game. I was on fire. I usually played centre midfield, and that night I couldn't do anything wrong. I was flying down the pitch and passing like a dream. I was so into the game that I forgot all about the time.

Then someone scored a goal that should have been disallowed. Things got heated, not with anger but with passion.

"He was offside," the goalie shouted.

"No way," said David. He was the forward who'd scored the goal. He had a tekky left foot and a great strike of the ball.

I got involved too, shouting that the goal was legit because it was my team who had scored. Then I looked around for the first time in what felt like hours. It was getting dark. The sky was purple and the streetlights were on. "Hey, maybe we should head home," I said. "Play more tomorrow."

The other kids agreed, so we left the cage. We weren't in any hurry, though, and we stopped at the corner near my house to talk about football stuff, like we always did.

"Who do you think Arsenal will buy this

season?" the goalie asked. "Do you reckon they'll get Ronaldo?"

"No way can they afford him, man."

Ronaldo was the most expensive footballer at the time. (The Brazilian one, not the Portuguese one.) Anyway, time flew by again and then I heard someone shouting my name, and they sounded angry.

It was my mum. She was striding towards us, with a face like thunder. My heart dropped. What had I done this time? But before I could ask, my mum was shouting at me. "Do you know what time it is? How dare you stay out so late? Do you have any idea how worried I was about you? And the rest of you! Your mums are worried sick too. Go on, get home the lot of you." Then she grabbed my ear and marched me home.

I was shocked. I'd never been in trouble like that, and I was angry and embarrassed at being shouted at in front of my mates. I thought it was unfair as well because my mum knew that it wasn't like me to stay out late. I normally came home whenever she told me to.

I thought about that night many years later in that changing room with the Under-10

Arsenal players. I could see the same passion and commitment on their faces. And I knew they probably got carried away and stayed out too late playing, like I had. I was older then, though, and I felt bad about making my mum worried that night, and I also knew that passion has to be controlled.

I'd realized that by keeping my passion under control I could focus it and make the most out of it. It is like holding a glowing light in your hand and pointing it. You can learn to apply it to big things, like a football match, or small things, like getting better at doing kick-ups. It's the same as any other emotion. It takes time to understand it and work with it. And, over time, I also became more aware of how my passion affected others, and I was more careful not to let it take over everything.

Loving football has made my life easier and more enjoyable, though. And I'm lucky to have a passion for music too. They both allow me to express myself and give me some escapism. When things aren't going right, I can get away from it all, either on the football pitch or with music.

Having a passion for something is a gift. It can mean that no matter what is happening in your life, you have an opportunity to leave any negativity behind and concentrate on something positive.

A passion can give you the chance to express yourself and feel good, as well as giving you energy and drive. You wake up happy each morning, because you want to enjoy your passion for another day. It will help you see a little bit of hope in every situation, no matter how down you might feel. And that is something very special.

YOUR ATTITUDE IS YOUR SUPER POWER

It can be pretty hard to stay positive when life throws you curveballs. I had a really hard time feeling upbeat when it came to leaving primary school. I don't know how you feel about school, but I liked it, or I mean I liked seeing my friends and playing football. And once I'd sorted out some of my issues with my big emotions (and Jamal), I felt like I was coasting. I had some pretty good teachers too and some great friends. From Year Three to Year Six, it was like I was relaxing in the back of a brand-new Mercedes S-Class, one of the smoothest cars ever. But then someone stepped on the brakes and the car stopped suddenly. I was pushed out of my seat and the seat belt pulled at my neck.

I was going to secondary school. Just the thought of it made me feel like I couldn't breathe. I would have to start all over again. It had taken me ages to make sure everyone at primary knew I was the best footballer. And even longer to be seen as one of the most popular kids. I didn't want to start again.

Plus, in Year Six, you're at the top of the school. Now I was being pushed back to the bottom. I was going to be a small fish in a big pond again. A huge pond, because secondary seems massive compared to primary. I wasn't looking forward to it at all. It didn't help that I wasn't going to the same secondary school as a lot of my friends. I'd wanted to, because I'd thought then it would all be fine. My friends knew me. They'd keep me going until everyone else knew me too – until I felt comfortable.

But I wasn't the one in control of which school I went to. My mum was. And because she was a teacher, she had all the inside knowledge about which schools would be the best for her son.

The school my friends were going to wasn't a very good one, in her eyes. Some of my cousins went there too, and they used to tell me about the fights that happened every afternoon: their school vs kids from schools in other areas that had come down for a scrap.

"You should have seen the mash-up at school today. Oh man," my cousins would say. "They were properly going for it. Even the teachers didn't know what to do."

"And that kid ended up in hospital. He broke his arm."

My mum wasn't having that for me.

But there was one school that we both agreed on. My best friend was going there and his sister was already there. There were certain grades I needed to get into the school, though, and I had to take a test. It was probably one of the few state schools that needed one.

A few weeks after the test, a letter arrived from the school. Mum and I opened it together. I was so nervous my hands were shaking. "Dear Mrs Rolle," it read. "We're sorry to inform you that we are unable to offer Leon a place at our school..."

I barely read the rest of the letter. I'd thought I wouldn't get in, but it was still a blow to see those words in black and white. I felt winded like someone had punched me. How was I going to make it through this transition from primary to secondary without friends or the teachers I knew to guide me?

And things got worse because my second and third choices turned me down too. So, I was in limbo. Where was I going? Who would my friends be? Who could I turn to? It got harder to focus on my future because all of a sudden it seemed further away. Like running for a bus you know you can't catch.

I thought maybe I'd have to home-school or something. I started not to care, to be honest. It was too much for me to cope with, so I stopped thinking about it.

Then my mum stumbled across a place. It was a religious school that was outside of my local area. A last resort. I wasn't happy.

Now, I can see that my mum really cared about me and had worked hard to find somewhere that she thought was good, and I could have learned something from it. But at the time all I could see was that this kind of place was so unfamiliar to me. I just thought, why am I going to some school where I know no one that is, like, 40 minutes from my house? I was angry that all my friends could walk to school, catch jokes with each other, and I had to look at them while sitting alone on a bus.

To make it worse, the school was in Tottenham and I was from Hackney. They had beef! I tried to tell my mum this but she wouldn't hear it.

"The school is a good one, with ethics and morals," she said. "I don't care about 'beef' and I don't want to hear anything about the streets!"

Which I thought was weird because it was the streets that had stopped her sending me to the local schools!

All of this was really hard on me. I felt like I had no control in my life. Do you ever feel like that? If you do, you'll know how much it hurts. Nothing was going the way I'd expected it to and it scared me. I started to worry about what was going to happen next, and I felt lost. Suddenly I didn't understand my situation. My feelings were all normal, but I didn't know that at the time.

Those six weeks between primary and secondary should have been a dream come true. No homework, and I could spend more time outside with my friends. Or playing my PlayStation. Or doing what I usually did, which was kicking a ball about, or messing about with music. Six weeks of playing football, hanging with friends and making music, imagine that. Sick.

But I couldn't enjoy it. I was too scared about what was coming next.

It wasn't just friends from school I would miss. It was the teachers too. (I wouldn't admit this at the time. We weren't supposed to say we liked teachers. I can now, though.)

There was one teacher I was super sad to be leaving: Mrs Jones. She treated me differently to all the others. Not because I was different, but because she was. She cared about every student and showed it in ways that were individual to each person in her class. She paid attention and never talked down to anyone. She never got tired of our questions, and you could actually have a conversation with her about things that had nothing to do with school or our work.

Mrs Jones set the standard for how teachers should be. So, yeah, I was sad when I had to leave her. I wish I'd been able to tell myself that if there was one Mrs Jones in the world, there would be another. There are billions of nice people out there and I was bound to find more like her. But at the time I wasn't thinking like that.

So, with all that going on, I was down. That summer didn't feel like six weeks; it felt like for ever. But, finally, it was the first day at my new school. I got up at 6 a.m., got dressed in my new uniform. It was dead: burgundy… All burgundy. I was not in a good mood.

And things didn't get much better after that. It took me a while to make even a single friend. Every day there was "beef" in the school. There were fights and grudges. Students would stare at you aggressively and when you looked back they would say, "What?"

They'd also hang around outside school. "Where you from?" they'd ask. Because it mattered if you weren't from their area.

I would lie, of course. But the question would drain me and make me feel like more of an outsider.

Eventually, I became cool with a kid from around my area. He was in a similar situation to me and we got along. But school was still rough. There was no Mrs Jones around to check in on me either. All the teachers were strict and stern. They were about authority with no compassion. I remember one maths class. I was messing around and this teacher just walked up behind me and smacked me on the neck with a ruler.

"Hey!" I shouted. "Don't do that!"

"You will not speak to me like that," he said.

That just made me madder.

I started screaming and swearing. He was shouting at me to stop, but I didn't care. I hated that school and I hated him. When I jumped on a table, he told me to leave.

"Fine," I shouted back. "I don't even need this place." And I stormed out.

I was so angry. I couldn't believe he'd hit me. But I was upset at more than just being whacked on the back of my neck. I was upset at how I'd been treated, and I was angry that I was at that school in the first place, which didn't seem much better than the ones near home.

When I got back to my house, I told my mum what had happened and she drove me straight back to the school. She was furious. She cussed all the teachers and then told me

I wasn't going back. It was halfway through the term, so I had to wait for the next one to start before I could go anywhere else.

Another fresh start. Things were out of my control again. It began to feel like a test that I was failing. I had no idea how to overcome this feeling of powerlessness. Was I even going to end up anywhere? And what would it be like? I'd have to make friends all over again. I felt down again, and I lost focus.

Even football training wasn't as exciting. It felt like I was losing a grip on my potential future in school and as a footballer. So, I started sneaking into one of my cousin's classes during the day. Imagine that: I'd left one school, I had free time, and I decided to *sneak into lessons* somewhere else. I was breaking rules to *enter* a classroom.

At the time, I didn't know why I was doing it. Looking back now, though, I think I just wanted some certainty. Kids went to school – that was what they did – and I wanted that too. It gave some order and structure to my life. It was about more than just seeing my friends and being bored at home. And it was so easy to get in. All you had to do was wear a jumper the same colour as the uniform and the teachers didn't care. The whole time I was there, no one noticed. I can see why my mum didn't want me to go there.

Eventually, though, we found another school. It was a place my mum approved of, and it was near football practice, so I was happy. And even though it was far from home, I was used to travelling by then. So, it didn't seem like a journey at all. Plus, the headteacher was one of those who go from school to school, changing them for the better. So, this felt like the right place for me.

This was around the time when things began to change for me, and this was the school where I eventually got the name Locksmith. (It came about because I got hold of a spare set of caretaker keys, which meant I could open any door in the school. So, I was the Locksmith.)

But it wasn't the last time I had to change schools. And it was certainly not the last time I had to deal with changes that were out of my control. Or that I wasn't ready for.

But during that whole experience I'd learned something. Too often it's easy to feel like things are happening to you and that you have no control over them. I felt like that often as a kid, but now I can see that the one thing I always had power over was my attitude.

I wish I'd had the positive mental attitude as a kid that I have now. (Or let's call it PMA, for short.) Because then anywhere my journey took me, I would have been able to look around at all the unfamiliar things and focus on being positive and get through it. I could have used my mind to find something to help me stay strong and confident. That would have felt like a superpower back then. Actually, it feels like a superpower now.

Had I kept positive, I would not have felt so sad over and over again. Changing schools was hard. Change by itself is hard. But it's all part of growing up and making your way through life. One step prepares you for the next ones.

The hardest moments become a little easier when you can see that it is just a moment. And beyond it there is something easier, or something to be learned and gained.

Everyone knows how to walk: you put one foot in front of the other without worrying about anything. I think we should treat life the same way. Trust yourself and remain positive that your soul will touch down and feel grounded. You are more than your struggles. If you stay positive, you are beyond them before they arrive. Keep going, stay strong, and you will get to the place that rewards you. It always comes. Just like it did for me.

YOU ARE NOT ALONE

It was the beginning of another world tour.

My alarm woke me up.

I got out of bed without closing my eyes again. I am still disciplined by the passion I had when I was younger. I love music and I love my band.

I washed and got dressed.

While I was having breakfast, my manager called me, like he always does before we go on tour. "Hey, Leon," he said. "How's it going? Shall I send a car for you?"

I said the same thing I say on every world tour: "No, thanks. I'm good."

"OK, see you at the airport." I could almost hear the smile in his voice. He knew I was going to say that, but he called me anyway, just to check in, because he's a good manager.

I got in the car and I drove to the airport. I listened to my tunes with the car window a little bit open.

I could hear the tunes from my playlist, but I could also hear and feel the cars next to me.

I was loving it. It made me feel at peace and got my head in the right space for what was coming up.

When I arrived at the airport, I said hello to everyone.

I shook hands with the people I see as my people.

I fistbumped the ones who are closer to me.

And I hugged those who are the closest to me. Those people are my band mates. We have toured the world together, won BRIT Awards and sold millions of albums as a group. How much more connected can you be?

But after we said hello, they whispered to me, "See you at the terminal." Because they know I like to be alone. And they respect that. And that's one of the key things about friendship – knowing what the other person needs and respecting it.

And that is pretty much the routine throughout the world tour. I do what I need to do and then I spend time alone. I have a family now, so I spend time thinking about them. (I miss them a lot when I'm away.) Or I listen to music. Sometimes I think about a way to improve my music or try and come up with a new melody for a song. I'm always trying to perfect my passion.

But I always smash it when I'm on stage. I force my way out of my loner personality so that I can entertain my fans. I guess some people might see all the time I spend alone as charging myself up before a show. And the best thing is my band mates totally get it. They embrace my desire to be alone without letting it affect our friendship, because they know it doesn't change my performance on stage or how I feel about them. But it wasn't always like this with the people around me. And I didn't always understand my need to be alone in the way I do now.

When I played for Arsenal's youth team, we would have long journeys on the coach to matches. For most players, this was the time to have fun. Everyone would be kidding around, laughing at the way a person ran or headed the ball. There would be laughs and screams. Everything was always exaggerated.

But it wasn't mean. The banter was all good fun. It meant we were in a good mood, and the coaches didn't mind because they knew it would be easy to turn that into positivity on the pitch and maybe a win on the day.

I knew all this was going on around me, but I hardly ever got involved. I would sit at the back of the bus with my headphones on, listening to the beats I had been making or tunes I wanted inspiration from. Sometimes I smiled at my team-mates when they pointed at me and expected me to laugh along with them. But I couldn't hear them. I could barely see them. And that's because I was locked in my own loneliness.

Being alone is not a negative thing. You can listen to your own thoughts and feelings more clearly when you're on your own. So, being by yourself can allow you to build a relationship with who you are. It can help you figure out what you want from your life too. And while I was sitting alone on those coach journeys, I was planning what I would do on the pitch. In my imagination, I would replay certain moves over and over again. I took free kicks in my mind and crossed the ball to my imaginary opponents. But because I was quiet, I would be asked about ten times by team-mates if I was OK. And I always said yeah. Because at the time I was. I enjoyed my own company, and I still do.

But, of course, like everything, there is another side to this too. Because sometimes you become a loner because you *feel alone*. You're not alone out of choice but because you think no one gets you or no one cares about you. You may not even realize that is what you are doing, and that can be damaging to you and those around you.

I think that was how I felt a lot as a kid, but I didn't know it at the time. It was partly because I was the middle child. There were six years between me and both of my sisters. That meant I didn't feel like I could relate to anyone in the house. Also, my dad didn't live with us. He was around me sometimes, but he was busy. He had more than one family, so he was in and out of so many different houses. Which all meant he didn't have time to help me relate to him or teach me anything. And as you know, this fuelled anger inside me but, also, it made me feel very lonely. Feeling alone and feeling angry were like two emotions holding hands for me.

I knew the anger was a problem, but I didn't think my loneliness was. Looking back at myself now, though, sitting on those Arsenal youth coaches, I can see that I had embraced being a loner but I didn't understand what it meant or why I was doing it. It took me some time to realize how being a loner and enjoying your own company aren't the same thing.

So, on this one particular day, when we arrived at the rival team's pitch, I jumped out of the coach and breathed in the fresh air. I was suddenly alive again and no longer the lonely zombie from the drive up. I started talking to everyone and making jokes.

It was cold that day so I was jogging on the spot to warm up. Breathing out the cold smoke of winter, I told everyone how many goals I was going to score ("three") and what skill I was going to do on the pitch. Then I did the skill with my feet without the ball.

My team-mates looked at me, confused.

"What?" I asked.

"Leon, mate, don't get mad," one said. The goalie, I think. His name was Pete. "But we don't get it. How are you so quiet on the coach and then so hyper out here?"

"Yeah, it's hard to keep up with you," the centre-back said.

"You can be well moody and then you expect us to be friends again," Pete said.

The whistle blew then so that was the end of the conversation. But I kept replaying what they'd said in my head. I don't even remember if we won or not that day, and I don't remember if I scored. All I remember is what my team-mates had said about me being moody and it being hard to understand me. Up until then I'd never thought about how me wanting to be alone affected other people. I hadn't really properly thought about how it affected me either, or why I was doing it.

When I got home that afternoon, everyone was there because it was a weekend. It was noisy. My sisters were running up and down the corridor, shouting and laughing. Seeing them together, playing and getting on, only made me feel more alone. They didn't even notice me come in, so I went upstairs to my room and shut the door. I felt sad and lonely and angry that no one in my family cared enough to see if I was all right. They didn't seem to care if I was home or not.

After what felt like hours, I went down to the kitchen to get a drink. My mum was at the table chopping something for dinner. I didn't speak to her. I was too caught up in my anger and my loneliness. I took the orange juice out of the fridge and went to drink it from the carton, but before I could put it near my mouth, my mum shouted my name.

"What?" I snapped back, thinking she was going to tell me off for drinking straight from the carton.

She flinched at my tone and I felt guilty, but I was angry and I didn't want to back down, so I crossed my arms defensively.

She sighed. "Leon," she said. "Sit down." She held up her hand to stop me protesting. "Just do it. Talk to me. What's wrong?"

I slumped into a chair just as one of my sisters came into the room. Oh, great, I thought, that's it now, I'll be ignored again. But my mum shouted "No! Out!" at her.

My sister eyed me as she left the room. She thought I was in trouble.

Mum looked at me again. In fact, she

stared at me without saying anything else for a long time. Five minutes went by but it felt like five hours. I couldn't take the silence any more.

"No one listens to me!" I shouted. "No one even cares if I'm here or not." I was shaking and I could feel the tears coming to my eyes. My hands were on the table and my mum reached over and put her own on top of one of mine. And as she did, I felt some of the anger and the loneliness seeping away.

We started talking. We talked about everything: how lonely I felt sometimes, but how I also liked being on my own, and how that affected other people, and how to handle that. I told her about the coach journeys to football matches and what my team-mates had said. And my mum listened and she held my hand the whole time. It felt like I was pouring out my emotions the way I did when I was playing football or listening to music.

And after I'd finished talking, I felt like a new person. How could I have felt alone with my family around me? My mum had been right there the whole time, and so were my sisters. I just needed to reach out and talk to them, and tell them how I was feeling.

Being alone isn't a bad thing. It can help you focus on your passion and learn new things without someone distracting you. It can make you comfortable with yourself and help you be independent. But it can make you sad or angry, like it made me angry, if you feel like you're alone all the time. And that can make you feel like no one cares about you. But that is never true.

I know it can be hard to see this. The tunnel you are in when you feel lonely is tough to escape. But the light isn't always at the end of the tunnel; it is all around it. We need to gather the strength to force our way through the barriers that create our tunnel and appreciate the light from people looking out for us. We need to recognize that there are people who care about us.

Feeling lonely as a child has negatively affected me as an adult. I still find it hard to talk about my emotions. It's hard for me to talk to you right now.

My mind still sometimes thinks that nobody cares. But my heart knows better. It knows that there will always be people to listen to me. And there will always be people who care about me. I don't have to be alone unless I want to be. And neither do you.

FIND YOUR TEAM

When I was fourteen, I thought I was doing great. I was finally at a school I was happy with. On top of this, I had these new shoes that no one else had yet. They were called Wallabees. The sole was really rubbery and soft, and the top was a smooth material. Sometimes they had cracks in them. It was the style. And in the middle of the shoe there was a gold square that said "Wallabees" or "W Shoe". That's how you knew they were real. And mine were.

I wore them with a Nike cap and a backpack that was attached to my coat. That was the icing on the cake. No one had ever seen a coat and bag in one.

All of this combined made people interested in me. Very quickly students started knowing who I was. Kids in the years below and above would chat to me in the corridors. (Even teachers and the caretaker knew me.)

"What's up?" kids would say, and "Where did you get that coat-bag from?", or "Oh my days, you've got Wallabees."

So, I'd say "Hey" and "Don't worry about where I got the bag. You, man, good, though, yeah?" Inside I was pleased, but I hid my smile because I felt I had to act tough.

And I thought I was the sickest boy in Year Nine.

But as time went by, I started to realize that, although people knew my name, they didn't talk to me that much. They would never spend time with me at lunch. They would talk to me for a few seconds then go back to their friendship group while I was still standing alone.

When I wasn't playing football, I sat by myself most of the time. My best friend was in the year above, so he had his own friendship group and he couldn't be around me all the time. I spoke to the caretaker a lot. And some of the dinner ladies. Especially the ones who lived near me. But I was lonely a lot. And I had time to think. I finally decided I needed to make more of an effort and stop trying to seem tough all the time. If I wanted to laugh and crack jokes with real friends like everyone else, I needed to do something differently.

Most of the kids who went to my school lived near one of my cousins in East London, so I started visiting him a lot. I thought he could help me make friends and be accepted by the people at school.

This was around the time that grime music was getting popular on estates. So, a lot of the people I met near where my cousin lived were into music the same way I was. I was getting more and more passionate about DJing and I felt connected to these people.

In the beginning, everyone called me "the boy from Hackney". I didn't mind. It was kind of like at school. I had to earn my place. I knew everything would work out in the end and I would be accepted and considered a friend. Which was what I wanted. I did have a slight feeling that some of the people I was chatting to every day did not have my best interests at heart. How could they? They didn't really know me because I was putting on a fake personality again, just like at school. But I wanted them to accept me and I thought this was the best way to do it.

Mostly, we hung around on street corners and on the steps of flats in the area. Apart from talking about music, we used to get up to mischief. Nothing serious, but we were bored, so we had to do things to entertain ourselves. I don't remember us ever getting into issues with the police or doing stuff that would get us into big trouble. Until one day when things became different.

On the day it all changed, the sun was shining and I was excited to get out of the house. Usually, my mum and I argued when I wanted to play out. But that day the only thing she said was "Have fun." That made me feel like this was going to be a good day.

The feeling continued as I went to the shop for sweets and came out to find the bus waiting for me. I had to change buses, but that one came straight away too. The bus driver smiled at me and nodded when I got on. I nodded back and felt even better about the day. All my friends were on the top deck of the bus, which never happened, even though we were all usually going to the same place. Everyone was excited and we were shouting over each other. For once, the driver didn't complain.

The day just kept getting better.

Me and a couple of other boys got off in an area we used to hang around in. The rest of the boys decided to go somewhere else first. We would meet them later. Chatting and laughing, we walked past the post office and job centre and then stopped in front of a pub.

"Hey, look," said one of the boys I was with. His name was Dave. He nodded at a group of men who were standing and talking outside the pub. One of them had left their phone on the table. "Looks like a nice one." Dave lowered his voice. "I'm going to grab it."

My heart caught in my throat. I didn't want to nick someone's phone. I'd never been involved in anything like that.

Before I could do anything, Dave was talking really loud and waiting for us to respond. I knew he was trying to create a distraction so he could take the phone.

The other boy – JJ – said something loud as well and then Dave darted forward, snatched the phone from the table and started running away.

So, I ran too. I didn't know what else to do.

There was a shout behind us. "Oi!" The men were coming after us.

Me, Dave and JJ ran faster, our feet pounding on the pavement. My heart was beating fast and I was scared. I didn't want those men to catch up with me. It felt like we were running for ever but eventually we reached the estate. It was quiet behind us and when I turned round there was no one there. The men had gone. I was shaking so hard, though. All three of us were. And then Dave said, "I didn't think we'd get away."

"They were fast, man!" said JJ.

"Not as fast as us!" Dave said. "We're the best."

And suddenly it felt like we were. It was like we had escaped this massive danger, and it brought us together. I felt like we'd survived something. I know that makes no sense as what we'd done was wrong, but we had this big important secret between us now. We felt like friends who had completed a mission and now we were brothers for ever. I think that shows how much I needed acceptance at the time. I was so blinded by it I couldn't see I wasn't being myself.

Dave put the phone in his pocket, and we decided to split up, in case the men caught up with us. I walked in one direction and the other two boys went off to sell the phone. I was still feeling like it was my day and that things were going my way. Sure, my friend had stolen a phone, but I felt like I could say he was my friend and he would agree. And that hadn't happened to me for a long time. I felt like I belonged. I ignored the voice that said my mum would be disappointed in me. But then something happened that opened my eyes completely.

The sun was still shining and I was still a little bit out of breath from running. I'd caught up with the rest of the group. Everyone was talking loudly and I was just listening. I was enjoying hearing all the voices speaking at once. It kind of felt like music. I focused on trying to hear one voice more than the others, like I was trying to find an instrument in a beat. I heard the voice say "Look!"

Everyone became silent and I turned around to look down the road. Walking towards us was the man whose phone we'd stolen and some of his mates. They all looked angry and one was carrying a baseball bat. I felt scared. Someone in our group shouted “Run!”

But for some reason I didn’t move, and suddenly I was the only one left standing in our spot.

When the men reached me, we started fighting. I hit two of them, and when I tried to get the third, he tackled me and forced me onto the floor. I was hitting him while he was on top of me and then the other three men started kicking me in my stomach. Every time they kicked me, I punched their friend. Then one of them raised the bat and brought it down on my thigh. Then he did it again. It hit my ankle, and the pain was immense. And I knew I had to get out of there before they hurt me more.

I got to my feet somehow and screamed at them so they would panic a little bit. They fell back when I shouted and as soon as I saw a gap between them, I ran through it.

I ran as fast as I could, only looking back once. The men who beat me up were not chasing me. But behind them I could see Dave and JJ. They were just standing there, chatting and laughing. And I realized that they'd seen everything and hadn't helped me. I was so shocked.

The adrenaline was running through my body so I couldn't think properly, but somehow I got on a bus and made it home. Just like at the beginning of the day, the bus was waiting for me when I got to the bus stop. I jumped on it and sat back in a seat on the bottom deck. I was a footballer, but I had never felt so out of breath.

When I got home, I said hello to everyone but no one looked round. I walked into the kitchen to get a drink. I felt a lot calmer. My adrenaline had nearly gone.

One of my sisters walked in. "What happened?" she asked.

I tried to shrug it off, but she kept on at me. "Something's definitely wrong," she said.

Eventually I told her I'd had a little fight, but it was nothing serious. I walked to the fridge. I could tell she was watching me, but I tried to ignore her. I didn't want to talk about it.

"If it's nothing serious, what's wrong with your foot?"

Until then, I knew my foot felt weird, but I didn't know why. When she asked me, it was like my ankle started crying for help. Suddenly I was in so much pain. I felt light-headed and I could feel the pulse in my leg. I collapsed on one of the kitchen chairs and my sister looked at my leg. She screwed up her face. "It's bad, Leon. We need to go to hospital."

"It's fine." I tried to shrug her off. I didn't want to make a fuss. I didn't want to tell my mum what had happened.

My sister stared at me for a few minutes, then she said, "Are you in trouble?"

I shook my head but I think she could tell I was lying. She didn't say anything else, just left the room. I heard her shouting up to our mum that she was taking me to her friend's house. "Back in a bit," she said. Then she came back into the kitchen. "Right," she told me. "You. Up. We're going to A&E."

I'd broken my ankle in two places and also broken my wrist. The doctor put my leg in a cast and a sling around my arm and sent me home. I told my mum it was a football injury and she believed me. My sister kept quiet too. I was glad. I didn't want my mum to know the truth. She had trusted me to go out in the morning and behave and I didn't want to disappoint her. I felt lost and upset and stupid.

At school the next week none of the kids I'd been with when I got beaten up even came to ask me how I was. I sat on the school steps at lunchtime, feeling sorry for myself, and watched all the other kids running around. Then I heard raised voices coming from the football cage. I hobbled over as best I could on my broken ankle. Someone had scored a goal and everyone was cheering. The sight of the footballers all hugging and shouting made me happy.

"Who scored?" I shouted.

One of the boys came over. It was a kid called Marc. We played football together a lot. He was a great tackler. "Hey, Leon," he said. "What happened to your leg?"

I was ashamed to tell the truth so I told him I fell when I was running for the bus. He laughed, but in a nice way, and then we started chatting about the Arsenal match at the weekend. Soon, a load of the other boys had come over. They were all asking about my leg as well. They wanted to sign my cast.

As I was standing there, laughing and chatting, it hit me. I had been chasing acceptance so much that I'd ended up running away from the people who already accepted me: my team-mates. We were like a family. We spent time together on coaches and had so much fun in changing rooms. Our football kits unified us, and everyone cared about one another. There were no selfish players.

In a football team, people know exactly who you are and what your position is. But I chose to ignore them and search for colours and stripes on the street. I learned a big lesson about friendship that day, one I wouldn't forget.

It's important to find people who make you feel good about yourself. After my experience with JJ and Dave, I started playing a lot more football in school and I worked on making some genuine friends. It was much easier than I thought it would be, because I didn't have to think about making an effort; it was just natural.

It was a huge relief to find that I could be me and people would accept me. I wish I'd realized sooner that I was already loved and accepted. And you are too. You just need to find your own people, like I did. Have the confidence to be yourself and you'll soon find your own team that believes in you and supports you.

DON'T FAKE IT

As you'll know by now, reading this book, I haven't always been comfortable being me. Growing up, I had big emotions, especially anger, and it took me time to deal with that and to be OK with who I am. A turning point in that journey came for me when I was in secondary school.

I'd got in with a local gang.

Looking back now, that wasn't a great idea, and even at the time I wasn't sure it felt like the right thing to do, but it happened anyway.

A boy in that gang was always staring at me. I didn't know him well. We didn't talk, but I knew his name was Mo, and I could tell he had a problem with me.

I don't know what I did to him. I think he was upset that everyone else had to do something to get into the gang and I hadn't. Maybe it was because the gang leaders thought

I was strong. Or cool, because I always had on nice clothes. Anyway, I managed to get into the gang by just hanging around with them and saying, "What are we doing today, guys?" And I think that annoyed this boy. And he kept staring at me until one day he decided to say something.

We were in a big group and the rest of the gang were smoking.

"How come Leon isn't smoking with us?" Mo asked. He wanted to test me.

Smoking was a big part of being in the gang, even though smoking is bad for you. I hated it and I never smoked. I didn't want to and I didn't think it was cool at all. The gang had offered cigarettes to me before, but I always turned them down. I told them I was an athlete and couldn't smoke. That was true but, also, I didn't want to smoke.

Maybe the fact that I was in the gang but didn't have to smoke annoyed Mo. That was the thing about gangs: to join them, you mostly had to do what they said.

No one took much notice when Mo shouted at me, so he did it again. "Oi, how come Leon's not smoking?"

This time everyone in the group heard, and they could all feel the tension. They were looking around wondering what would happen. But I wasn't scared.

"I'm an athlete," I said, like I had all the other times, and I turned to talk to someone else.

Then, all of a sudden, Mo grabbed me. He held my head and tried to force the cigarette into my mouth. I pushed him away and then I punched him in the chest. I did it without thinking. I was growing up and I didn't like fighting any more. Also, I knew he felt bad for what he'd done. He cared a lot about being in the gang and what people thought of him. Anyway, even thinking all of that, I still hit him, and he fell back and landed on the floor.

Everyone started laughing, and I felt worse for him.

But it got me thinking more about what I was doing in this gang.

I'd only been in it about five months. I'd joined because I wanted to see what was so interesting about it. Everyone in school respected the gang and was scared of them.

But did I really want to be with people like that?

To be honest, it was a bit boring too. We would just hang around places on the playground or just outside of school trying to look cool. We talked a little bit but not a lot. I didn't even hang around with them every day because I had football and my team-mates were my real friends. I had learned that and always remembered it. More and more, I wondered what I was doing. Then something happened that made my mind up.

I was walking out of my last lesson. I'd had to stay behind for a little longer because the teacher wanted to talk to me. "Leon," she said. "I'm so happy with the work you've been doing. You focus in class, even though I know this isn't your favourite subject. That's so great to see. You should be really proud of yourself."

I was smiling when I left the classroom because I felt like I'd come a long way from the angry kid who used to shout and throw chairs, and I was thinking about football too. I was getting better at that as well.

I decided that I was only going to play

for an hour after school that night so I could get home around the same time as my mum. I wanted to tell her what the teacher had said to me. I liked spending time with my mum.

But when I walked out of the school's main entrance, there was a group of people standing around someone. I was on the top step so I could see over their heads.

A girl was in the middle of the group. She had her head down and some kids were shouting at her. I couldn't see who it was, so I pushed through the group to the front. My heart sank when I saw some of the gang there. They were shouting at the girl and telling her to show them her hand. I recognized her then.

She was in my year, but in a different class, so I would see her around, in the playground and on the way to lessons, and people would talk about her because she always had her sleeves pulled down over her hands.

The rumour was that one of her fingers was missing. I knew some people in the gang thought what she did with her sleeves was weird and they wanted to know for sure if she had all her fingers. For me, it was none of their business. Everyone should leave this girl alone.

One of the gang saw me then. A guy called Sam. He called me over. "Go on, Locksmith. Tell her to show us her hand." When I didn't react, he got right up in my face and jabbed me in the chest. "I said I want to see her hand."

"Or what?" I said.

Sam stared at me but didn't speak. He didn't need to. There were loads of people from the gang there and I could tell that this was a test. I'd refused to smoke to be part of the gang, and if I didn't do this I'd be out.

I stood still for what felt like a long time but was probably only a few seconds. I thought about Mo trying to make me smoke and about a girl who'd become addicted to cigarettes because of the gang. And I remembered Dave and JJ, who'd made me steal that phone with them and then not stood up for me when I got attacked.

I was sick of doing things that other people wanted me to do. I wanted to be my own person. And I knew it was wrong to pick on this girl. I've always hated bullies and I wanted to stand up for her.

"Leave her alone, man," I said. "It's not even funny. Just move."

Everyone looked at me like their jaws were on the floor.

Sam shoved past me. "We're done," he said.

The others walked away too, even the girl they'd been picking on ran out of the school gates without a word.

I stood there alone, wondering what had happened. Honestly, I thought someone was going to say congratulations to me. I thought I would be praised for doing the right thing. But no one cared. The gang was finished with me and the girl didn't even say thank you.

For a minute, I wondered what I'd done.

I walked home thinking about everything. And I realized that I didn't care about being in the gang any more. I'd never really wanted to be in it in the first place. I didn't want to do stuff because other people told me to. I wanted to be my own person.

And I knew I had done the right thing, sticking up for that girl. And that felt good. I was happy. I was me and I felt calm within myself, like lying in a warm bath.

I went home and had tea with my mum and decided from then on, I always wanted to be me. And it was a relief. It meant I didn't have to pretend any more.

Sticking up for what's right can feel hard and scary. But it can feel good too. Standing up for that girl at school and leaving the gang felt great. I went home feeling calm and happy that day.

From then on, I decided to be me and to stand up for what I believed in, even when it was difficult. And I want you to have the confidence to do that too. I want you to be proud of yourself and the choices you make, and that means respecting and caring for others as well as yourself.

BELIEVE
IN
YOUR
FUTURE

At sixteen I could see nothing except the Beautiful Game and being the best at it. I gave my soul to football. I thought about it every night and day. Everything else took a back seat. Even the girls I liked could only get my attention by playing football with me. I had tunnel vision. And why not? I was good at football, and I played for the best team in the world: Arsenal. It was the team I supported too. Can you imagine that? It felt amazing.

Life was good. I wasn't getting into trouble, and school was OK. I hadn't been expelled. There was no stress over friends or beef or anything like that. It was a great time for me. And, on top of all that, I was being considered for Arsenal's Youth Training Scheme (YTS). Getting in meant you could make it into the first team and maybe one day live the dream of playing at Highbury, which was the Arsenal stadium at the time. I don't think they have those schemes any more, but back then it was a big deal. It was the dream and I knew I would make it. I was good, all my coaches knew it. And so did my team-mates.

I only had one problem. And that was my temper.

I won't lie; I was aware of it. Like I've said before, I was keeping it under control. Most of the time. But football gets passionate. Someone misses an easy pass or does something stupid on the ball, and I'll get annoyed. Players getting greedy and trying to shoot when I'm open? Especially when they're not even that good. (Or not as good as me.) Of course, I'll get angry.

But it wasn't just the players I used to argue with. It was the coaches, or just one coach really, who didn't like me, even though he rated my skills. We used to butt heads all the time. I'd be shouting at him from the pitch and he'd shout back from the sidelines.

What can I say? That's football. And I should not have taken anything personally. But there was something about this one coach that made me feel uncomfortable. Yeah, we'd argue. But he'd act a certain way towards me even after the games. He never left anything on the pitch. So, when it was my time to be considered for the YTS, I was praying that this coach would not be involved in the picking.

On the day I got to hear whether I'd got in or not, I walked up the corridor to the office, and I remember taking my time. I looked a bit scruffy; I can't lie. I was sweating a bit. My knees had dirt on them, my laces were untied and my shirt wasn't tucked into my shorts. There were bits of dirt under my fingernails.

I didn't feel very good about myself. It was like there was something inside me preparing me for bad news. But you can never be fully prepared for bad news, so part of me was still hopeful. A bit of self-belief was still alive inside me. I was still hoping that the coach I butted heads with wouldn't be there.

I opened the door to the small office, and the first person I saw inside was him. As I put my bag down and sat on the chair, the hope was fading out of me. I can't really remember what they said to me. I was only waiting to hear one thing. And then the head coach said it. "Leon, we are not taking you on for a YTS." And everything went black. I didn't hear anything else. All I heard again and again were his words. All my other senses disappeared. The only thing that was real were those words.

I felt my confidence drip out of me. It was like someone had poured water into my head and it swept away any self-belief I had. And what was filling up the empty space was anger. I could feel it. But I didn't want any of the coaches to see it. Especially *him*.

Without even letting them finish what they were saying to me, I picked up my bag and left. As I made it into the corridor, I heard one word: "Typical."

And I know who said it. By storming out, I had proved him right.

I stopped for a moment. I wanted to go back and scream at them. Didn't they know what this meant to me? On the team, we used to hear stories about players being denied the YTS and then begging for it, crying and refusing to leave. One of the players cried so hard that his parents had to come and get him. And then the parents started crying and begging.

Football was life to a lot of us. So, I felt like my life was over, or ruined anyway. I really wanted to throw everything in that room. But I couldn't give them any more of myself. They had already taken my confidence and my pride. I wasn't going to give them my anger too. So, I took a deep breath and kept on walking. I felt depressed. I almost felt like I didn't know who I was any more.

Believing in yourself is never easy, and I felt like football had given me so much confidence. Real confidence, not the fake self-confidence I wore as a mask at parties when I was the one dancing on the table. Because you can't fake it on the pitch. How would you ask for the ball? Or tackle, or do one or two skills, or even shoot the ball, if you weren't confident in your ability? It was an essential part of the game. And now football had destroyed my self-belief.

After that, I felt depressed for a long time. It was like my best friend had one day decided he wanted nothing to do with me. I had no one to talk to about how I felt either. No one in my family was interested in football, so I had to deal with the pain by myself. And

I was done with football. I couldn't even play a simple five-a-side. I sometimes felt sick just looking at a ball.

And then there was school. I say school but, really, I was finished with it. GCSEs were done, so the only thing left was to pick up our results.

Going to school to get them reminded me of that walk down the corridor to the office at football. But this time I didn't feel nervous. I felt calm. Because although I didn't pay much attention in school, I would always study for exams and do well. I'm one of those people who have an "almost" photographic memory. I can study the day before and remember most of what I read. This isn't a good way to study, but it worked for me. My grades were always decent, even though I did the bare minimum to get by. And this always annoyed my teachers, one teacher in particular.

On results day, I was late and everyone else was already outside talking about their grades. Some of my mates called out to me: "Hey, Leon! What's up, man?"

I nodded a hello at them, but I kept walking. I wanted to get my results by myself.

There were about five teachers out there too. “You’re late,” one said.

Another – the one that never liked me – said, “The receptionist has gone home. You’ll have to wait for your results.”

The other teachers laughed.

Yeah, right, I thought, but I knew why he was making jokes at me. I was a naughty kid and once I’d locked him in a cupboard in his classroom, and even though he couldn’t prove it was me, deep down, he knew. He’d probably heard me laughing as he was knocking on the door and asking the students to let him out. And I was the first one he’d called to the head’s office when another teacher finally got him free. So, yeah, he didn’t like me very much.

I knew he was trying to make me look stupid, so I kept walking into the school reception area.

Of course, the receptionist was still there. I don’t remember her name, but she was always kind to us kids. She smiled at me as she handed me the results envelope. I smiled back, but inside I was annoyed with that teacher. Why make a joke that wasn’t even funny?

After I'd picked up my results, I walked back outside. The results were in a brown envelope, and I thought about opening it then and there but decided not to. It was my business. I would take it home and open it with my mum. If my grades were bad, I could apologize to her straight away.

So, I put the envelope in my pocket and walked back to where all the other students were. Again, some of them shouted out to me – "Leon, tell us what you got, mate!" I ignored them. I wanted to go home and look at my results in quiet.

I was about to walk out of the school gates when I felt a hand on my shoulder. "Leon."

I turned to see who it was and it was the teacher who'd never liked me, the one who'd made the joke about the receptionist. I tried to keep walking, but he said, "Wait, slow down."

"No, man. I need to get home," I said. School was over; he wasn't my teacher any more and I didn't have to talk to him. Plus, I knew his reasons for wanting me to slow down were not good.

"Leon! I asked you to wait. I want to talk to you."

"I'm in a rush," I said, trying to get past him.

Before I could leave, he got down, got close to my ear and whispered, "You're never going to amount to anything."

At first, I was surprised he said that to me. It was like hearing a teacher swear. I was even a bit excited to hear his human side. But then the meaning of the words kicked in. And how he said it, with so much venom.

Shocked and upset, I sat on a low brick wall near school and thought back to that coach and the YTS rejection and I thought about what this teacher had just said to me. I wanted to understand why it felt like people wanted me to fail.

And suddenly it clicked. They didn't believe in me. They had never believed in me. And because of that they wanted me to fail, to prove themselves right. But I didn't want to fail. So, the only solution was that I would believe in myself, even when no one else did. I was not going to be beaten.

Energized, I jumped up from the wall and started walking to the bus stop. Something was rising within me. My body began to feel full. It was self-belief mixing with anger and determination. My confidence was returning.

I was shaking my head from side to side while I was walking. I was saying no to the world's low expectations of me. When I got to the bus stop, I stopped shaking and I looked into the distance. But I wasn't looking for the bus; I was looking at my future. I was filled with determination to succeed. To prove wrong everyone who didn't think much of me. And I knew I could do it. I believed in myself.

When I was growing up, there were a lot of people who didn't believe in me. And that hurt me. But it also made me strong. It made me determined to succeed, not for them, but for myself. And you can succeed too. Don't believe anyone who tells you otherwise.

Start believing in yourself and your future now, and don't let anyone try to take it away from you.

EVEN SUPER HEROES FAIL

There is a lot of pressure on you when you're a kid. From a young age, you're watched and tested. A lot. You're asked to do SATs and then GCSEs and A levels. And that's just at school. Outside of education, you have family and friends, sometimes girlfriends or boyfriends as well, who all expect something of you. And added to all this for me was sport. Football, mostly. (My first love.)

At football academies, there's a lot of pressure on you from really young. You can sometimes be picked for academies when you're only around seven. And from that point, you're taught to win. And that means you're scared to fail. Because failure can often mean you lose an entire game. And if you lose often, you know there is a chance you won't make it into the Under-16 squad.

So, you put pressure on yourself, and the coaches and other players put pressure on you too. If a shot is off-target, or a pass doesn't connect the way it should, you feel like you've failed. (Sometimes it can feel like the end of the world for something so small.) And your coach will remind you that you failed. Well, the bad ones will. And there are a lot of them, in and out of football.

I don't think it's fair that young players are made to feel like that, but football is a hard game and, as a player, you have to get used to criticism. It's not right, but it's the way it is in the game. My football coaches would say, "If you can't handle the way I talk to you, then how will you handle the crowd? A crowd will boo you and scream abuse at you. They will be a lot worse than anyone at the training ground."

That makes a kind of sense. But, in reality, instead of preparing me for failure, they made me scared of it. I was convinced for a while that any kind of failure should be avoided. Avoided at all costs. Because it would lead to heartbreak and feeling like your whole life is meaningless. Imagine that kind of life for a young boy. I might as well have locked myself in my bedroom for good.

I felt low for a long time after I didn't get into the Arsenal YTS. It felt like I'd been rejected by the one thing I thought was my destiny. But, eventually, I was able to find my self-confidence and I did start playing football again.

By then secondary school was over so I decided to join the college team. I knew I'd be picked. I'd just come from Arsenal, remember. C'mon. My confidence was definitely back by then. And I became part of the first team. But I still had to go to lessons and pass exams, and that felt like another failure waiting for me. I can't lie to you: at this point, I was still scared of what that could do to me. So, I decided to study a bit more than I used to.

One afternoon I went to the IT room with a friend to do a bit of revision. And there was a girl there. We started chatting and, eventually, we became friends. After that we used to hang out a lot. She was cool. And I could talk to her about anything. One time I told her that I was thinking about joining the army.

"Why?" she asked.

I shrugged. I hadn't given it a lot of thought. I'd just always assumed that if

I didn't make it playing football, I would join up. To be honest, I wasn't 100 per cent sure it was what I wanted to do, but the feeling of failure was nagging at me. I felt that if I was tougher and had military training, I would be less likely to fail at anything again. I don't know if that makes sense, but it made sense to me.

She looked at me for a long time. Concern was written all over her face, and I didn't get why.

"What?" I said. "What's wrong with me joining the army?"

"There's nothing wrong with it. I just don't think it's for you." I could tell she was getting emotional.

"Why's it not for me? Am I not tough enough?" That fear of failure was pushing at me again.

"No, it's not that. It's..." She drew in a deep breath and turned to face me. "Leon, are you trying to run away from something?"

"No way!" I was getting a bit angry then. What was she trying to say?

She put her hand on my arm. "Leon. I'm not trying to make you mad. I just think you're meant for something different. Open your eyes and look at what is right in front of you."

I blinked. *She* was right in front of me. And then I got it. She was telling me that the army wasn't my only option. I had other choices, including choosing to stay and spend more time with her. And that made me feel good, because I liked her.

But it was about more than that. She was telling me it was OK to take a risk on not knowing how something would turn out. And that meant I didn't need to do something I wasn't completely sure about because I was scared of doing anything else, and because I was scared of failing.

She kept talking for a long time after that, about all the stuff I could do with my life. And I listened to every word. After that day, I knew she could convince people of anything. I'd thought my mind was made up. And then suddenly it wasn't, because of her and what she'd said to me.

Until that moment I didn't understand that failure is part of life and there is nothing you can do to escape it. Even superheroes can't always achieve their goals, but they come back stronger. That's what makes them super; that's what makes them heroes. The key is to learn from mistakes and failure.

And failure is not always bad. In fact, it might not be a failure at all but just a way for you to improve at something or move towards something else. Something even better.

For instance, if I hadn't been rejected by the Arsenal YTS, I would not have become a global superstar. I also would not have ended up at that college talking to that girl who told me that the army wasn't my only option and later became my wife and the mother of my children.

I have told the story of how I met my wife many times. I use it to inspire and give hope. We met after my low point, and she helped me to understand that everything would be OK.

As an adult, I'm able to take a lot from people and life and not let it break me down. I like to think that we can take everything that happens to us and turn it into something positive. (We can take an L and turn it into a capital W; it's just about connecting the dots in a different way.) That doesn't always happen immediately and it can take a long time to accept that not achieving something was actually a good thing for you.

I try and see all challenges as a way to learn and develop myself. If I win or lose, succeed or not, it's all about learning. Every opportunity in life is a way to get better at what you do.

Maybe you can use that thinking too and learn not to worry about failing or making mistakes. They are a part of life and are what makes you the person you are.

YOU ARE STRONGER THAN YOU THINK

For me, human beings are a lot like ships. We're not meant to stay on the safest of shores, or seas, or harbours, but to venture out on adventures, so we learn that we can withstand the toughest of shores and waves and oceans. If we are willing to try and to dig deep, we have the ability to push our boundaries and to reach territory within ourselves that we didn't even know existed.

I honestly think that believing in yourself and your own strength is the most important thing you can do. You are stronger than you think; you just need to get out of your comfort zone and try.

Going on the TV show "SAS: Who Dares Wins" is a prime example of me jumping out of my comfort zone. In case you don't know it, the show puts contestants through a series of skills that are supposed to match the secret selection process of the SAS (the British

Army's Special Air Service). SAS training is known for being the ultimate test of physical and mental endurance.

So, unsurprisingly, the last 36 hours of the show were probably some of the toughest I've endured in my life. The directing staff demanded that the show be as authentic as possible. That meant no one on set talked to you: not the camera people, not the audio team. And you had no contact with the outside world at all. You literally had yourself and the other recruits to rely on.

Also, you were surviving on around 800 calories a day (basically three small portions), which is not a lot, especially if you're doing the level of physical exertion we were. Plus, sleeping was a myth! On the show, like in real SAS training, the trainers don't want you to be relaxed enough for sleep. They want you to feel uncomfortable because they want to see what you're made of deep down inside. They want to know what you're capable of when you're at your most sleep- and food-deprived and broken down.

It's pretty tough! (Who am I kidding? It was easily the toughest thing I've done in my life.)

So, in those last two days, I was beyond exhausted. I just wanted to lay my head down and get some sleep. So that's what I did, and it turned out to be a big mistake.

I was in my bunk, dozing, when suddenly a flash-bang was thrown into the room. There was no heads-up, no warning. But I was out of there like a shot. You would have thought Usain Bolt was in the room to see the way I shifted. I grabbed my already packed bag and I was the first out of the door, out of the barracks and up the mountain. I ran away as fast as I could from the sounds of guard dogs and the "enemy" chasing us. (The show is set up with tasks, and the last one is that you have to outrun an unknown enemy.)

At the top of the mountain, I took a minute to re-evaluate. I was in shock. I kept thinking what just happened? I couldn't believe how quickly I'd reacted to that situation, and it made me wonder where this soldier-like instinct had come from. I could only think it went all the way back to when I was younger.

I've always been happy to go out of my comfort zone, and that is because of my passion for football. Because I wanted to be the best, I pushed myself to train harder, better and more often, even if it was uncomfortable or difficult. I got up early every day so I could practise before school and I never missed a training session.

I trained hard off the pitch too. I remember going for a run at 5 a.m. on my twelfth birthday, because I knew that was the only time I could go that day. It was winter and freezing cold. My mum wanted to know what I was doing up and where I was going. "Leon, it's the middle of the night. Go back to bed."

I ignored her. I knew I had to train every day to be the best on the pitch; I was determined to succeed at my passion.

A lot of this drive came from looking at my heroes. I loved the *Rocky* films when I was a kid (you probably haven't even heard of them!), but I also had real-life heroes, like the footballer Ian Wright. He was someone I really looked up to. On tough days, at home or on the football pitch, I'd think of him and everything he'd gone through to become a professional footballer. I liked to think that there were similarities between us. We were both from London (me from the east and him from the south). We were both lovable, hot-tempered and talented, or so I thought, and I would try to mimic him in everything I did. I wanted to be him.

And it was stories like his that inspired me and made me believe that if you wanted to achieve your goals, you had to have an unapologetic desire, will and determination to succeed. And that meant pushing yourself out of your comfort zone.

So, it was ingrained in me from very young to stick to something, even when it was hard and uncomfortable, or even impossible! I think all of that put me in a good place for the "SAS" show because it allowed me to be comfortable out of my comfort zone without me having to think about it.

So, there I was: on top of a mountain in the middle of the night. My heart was pounding; there were sounds of dogs barking and people shouting all around me. I'd had no sleep, and now me and the other recruits had to use our rubbish map-reading skills to get to a prearranged meeting point. It was a low point. I just wanted to go to bed, but I was determined not to give up. I never let anything beat me.

So, I got my head down and I did what needed to be done. It took us nearly twelve hours. There was some boat travel, but the majority was on foot, travelling up and down mountains in the worst Scottish weather you can imagine, and the terrain was unforgiving. I remember now how my quad and calf muscles burned like fire.

But I made it, and when I was told I'd passed – you don't win SAS training; you survive it! – I was like "You what?" I just didn't believe it. When the news finally sank in, I didn't have the energy to celebrate. I broke down in tears. My whole body hurt. My nails were black from crawling up hills; I couldn't feel my hands or my toes. But I felt proud of myself. I'd achieved something. I'd stepped way out of my comfort zone and I'd survived.

That was the real victory for me.

You don't need to do SAS training to prove your strength. You don't need to get into a football training scheme or become a rock star. You prove it every day when you keep your dreams in your mind, and you aren't afraid to try things, just because they might not go exactly as you planned. That's life and you can't control it.

Life is a whirlwind of emotions, and it's a rollercoaster ride that never ever keeps you comfortable. And, honestly, I've learned the most about myself when things haven't gone to plan or when I've been far out of my comfort zone.

Believe in yourself, don't be afraid to make mistakes and then you will be capable of anything.

NEVER
GIVE
UP ON
YOUR
DREAMS

I never gave up on my dreams of becoming a professional footballer or global superstar, even when I was at my lowest. That was probably mad because the odds of making it as either are so low. Some would even say impossible. I'd say around 99.9 per cent of young footballers are rejected by their mother club before they are sixteen. And the odds of making it as a music star...? Well, even lower!

But I didn't care about stats, and I didn't care about the odds being against me. That knowledge just filled me with more ambition and more drive to prove myself to those that didn't have faith in me.

It wasn't always easy to keep going, but I was used to working hard and things not always going right. In fact, I've noticed a correlation between things going negatively in my life and me playing better football or making better music. I'm not saying I don't play well or have good shows when I'm feeling happy, just that some of my most elite performances, some of my best shows, have come when I felt like I was fighting for something.

For me, football and music are the same in that they are an opportunity to leave negativity behind and concentrate on something positive. As a kid, I would always gravitate to them as an outlet from everyday life. Football has always been my first passion – I've never made any secret of that – but I loved making music from a very young age too. And music was always there for me, especially when football wasn't kind, like when I didn't get into the YTS.

I don't know what my life would be like without music. Music is everything. It's a form of creation, a form of expression, a form of escapism. Sometimes I don't give it enough credit for saving me from going out on the street and letting out all this negative energy that I had in a bad way.

There were people in the same position as me who didn't have music, or any passion to keep them focused, and they got into crime. You can go down a right or a wrong path.

So, even though DJing was hard for me at the beginning, I never gave up on it. I was able to transfer the intense passion I had for football to music, and I practised a lot.

I started playing decks when I was very young, about eleven or twelve years old. When my mum got me my first pair, I became obsessed with them. I remember trying to mix these two records together for, like, six hours a day, going back and forth to the point that my mum would say, "You're going to make me hate Anita Baker, you're going to make me hate Marvin Gaye, and it's just the same tunes. Can you not pick another tune?"

I'd say, "These tunes don't match up, Mum, so I need to practise how to do it and I need to get good at it."

Then every week I would go to a local record shop and I would spend the twenty quid my mum gave me for school lunches on vinyl. (I would have to sweeten up the dinner staff at school to give me a free lunch, or pack one, just to survive because you can't eat records. Obviously.) Then I would put those two records on the decks and mix them for hours until the following week came when I'd spend that week's dinner money on new tracks. And I'd mix those.

It drove my family crazy because it would be the same tunes going over and over again, but all that practice, for hours and hours, stood me in good stead for the future. But despite all that, DJing didn't always go the way I wanted it to, because you can't plan for everything. Life just happens.

I remember my first night doing a set on a pirate radio station. One of my cousins had set it up for me. She was an MC and we'd often mix together, so she knew I was good. (Pirate radio was illegal but it was, like, our internet back then. It was a way for a new DJ to get noticed.)

I must have been about fourteen, and I was massively nervous, because I felt like this was my big break. But when I arrived at the studio, it all started going wrong. The place wasn't what I expected. The sound from the stations always came out clear and clean on my radio, so I just expected the sets to be recorded in a pristine studio, all soundproofed up and glossy, with all the best equipment there. But that was not the reality.

Instead, when I got there, I was staring at a busted-up door, next to a dirty-looking restaurant. Inside were these mouldy stairs. So, there I am, this fourteen-year-old, walking up two flights of dirty stairs with this vinyl box that weighed a ton and was doing my back in and I eventually got up to a manky room lined with mattresses (for acoustics and soundproofing, although I don't think they did the job). Oh yeah, and the decks were abysmal. In my head, I was thinking how am I going to do the set on these. I'd never DJed on these types of decks before, and I had no clue how to use them.

I told myself to pull it together. I had a great set planned and some sick tracks. I would be fine. But the vinyl kept jumping up because the needle was dusty and I couldn't get the mix to sound the way I wanted it to. Then these text messages started coming through from listeners saying, "This DJ is rubbish. Get this DJ off. He's wack."

It was horrible. I kept thinking this is the equipment; this isn't me.

But I couldn't tell anyone that, and it was heartbreaking, because I felt this was my chance to make a name for myself and I was blowing it.

I was gutted for a long time after that. But, you know, looking back now, I can see it wasn't such a big deal. I had other shots. Things don't always go your way, so you have to live and learn and just keep plugging away and trying to reach those heights again.

In the entertainment business, you soon realize there are more lows than there are highs. I know it doesn't seem that way from the outside, but that's because the highs get seen by your audiences and your lows get seen by no one but yourself and you have to deal with them alone. One of the things that has got me through is my belief that you've got to get comfortable with being uncomfortable. It's in those uncomfortable situations that you learn so much about yourself.

Also, my band mates in Rudimental are a big factor in keeping me grounded and on track, despite the tough times. We were fortunate to grow up together from a very early age, and we're like family. There's four of us in the band: me, Amir, Kesi and Piers. I've known Piers and Kesi pretty much all my life.

Rudimental started without us knowing that it was going to be Rudimental. In the beginning, we were pretty hard to categorize because we were a group of music producers at a time when producers didn't really get the credit or recognition they deserved. We didn't want one singer, or rapper, because we liked the thought of working with multiple artists. We kind of broke the mould in that respect, but it took us a long time to get noticed.

There were times when I spent hours and hours outside record label offices trying to get our music heard, but we got no responses, nothing – just rejection after rejection. I couldn't get a coffee or a meeting at any of those record labels, even the small ones. They didn't want us, not because we didn't sound good but because our faces didn't fit.

But it didn't matter to us. We knew in our hearts that it was going to happen. It was just a matter of opportunity. It was *when* rather than *if*. So, we kept plugging away, spending hours in the studio at night after work and DJing in clubs. I won't say it wasn't hard or disheartening, especially when we handed out a CD, only to see someone throw it away. I kept telling myself, *Don't give up. These heartbreaking moments will come good.* The dream of playing main stage at Glastonbury kept me motivated and inspired.

Then one night in the studio we created this song called "Feel the Love". I remember the feeling when we made it. We looked at one another and said, "This is it. That's the one."

"Someone's going to find us, man," I said.

To be fair, we had a moment like that every week. But that song felt special, and eventually it was our big break, although it sat on the hard drive for another two long years before we found the right vocalist and got it off to the music labels. But then it went round like wildfire. It went to Number One and allowed us to make more and more music.

I look back now and I think, what if I'd given up on my passions? Imagine if I'd stopped believing in myself when I got kicked out of the academy. Or after that rubbish first set on pirate radio. Imagine if I'd decided to give up when I was eight years old and got frustrated when I didn't know how to do something.

If I'd given up then that would have become a habit for me, and all those dominoes, those pillars that make me who I am today, would have toppled over. And I wouldn't be talking to you now, and none of this would be happening.

If I could tell you one thing it would be don't give up. Hold onto your dreams. Keep them alive for as long as you can, because they are important and they are special.

They are who you are and, so long as you're trying and working hard, you never know when they might come true. And if you don't make it in the end, then that's OK too.

I didn't make it as a professional footballer, but something even better came along for me, and it will for you too.

It's about that big journey on the way. That's an experience. You can't be taught that; you have to learn that for yourself. And that's the most important thing.

IT'S THE JOURNEY THAT COUNTS

Thanks for reading this book. I hope it's helped you understand that it's not the successes that make you who you are, but how you deal with everything that life throws at you. I wouldn't be where I am now without the highs and the lows.

Here are some thoughts to take with you.

1. Getting angry or crying is normal, but looking at your emotions and why you react the way you do can help you understand yourself better and make new or difficult situations easier to deal with. Talking to people you trust about how you feel can help too.

2. Have a passion or an outlet that allows you to express yourself and be who you truly are. Then no matter what's

happening in your life, you'll have a place to leave any negativity behind and concentrate on something good.

3. Keep going, stay positive, and you will get to the place that rewards you.

4. You are not alone. There are people around you who love and care about you.

5. Find your own people, your own team, who believe in you and support you.

6. Don't be afraid to stand up for yourself and what's important to you.

7. Believe in yourself and in your future.

8. Failure is not always bad. In fact, it might not be a failure at all but just a way to move you towards something else. Something even better.

9 You are stronger than you think; you just need to get out of your comfort zone and try.

10 Hold onto your dreams because they are special, and you never know when they might come true.

Most of all, remember: life is an experience that you can't be taught; you have to learn it for yourself. And it's the journey that counts, because that's what makes you who you are.

Take care,

Leon Rolle
Locksmith from Rudimental

ABOUT THE AUTHORS

Double or Nothing Productions

Leon Rolle is better known by his childhood name of Locksmith. Born and raised in Hackney, London, Locksmith formed worldwide platinum-selling UK music band Rudimental with three childhood friends in 2010. Since then, the group has performed in sell-out venues around the world, achieved two UK Number One albums and three UK Number One singles. The group has also won a BRIT Award for Single of the Year.

As well as being a talented musician, Locksmith is a skilled footballer. He was affiliated with a number of top UK clubs as a youngster, and he continued to play semi-professional football as an adult for the likes of Haringey Borough and National League teams Barnet, Dagenham & Redbridge and, up until recently, Braintree Town. He is still a keen footballer, valuing not only the physical benefits but the positive impacts on his mental wellbeing.

Stuart Simpson for Penguin 2020

Derek Owusu is an award-winning British writer, poet and podcaster. He grew up in Suffolk and London, and his debut novel for adult readers, *That Reminds Me*, won the Desmond Elliott Prize. He also edited and contributed to *Safe: 20 Ways to Be a Black Man in Britain Today*.

We'd love to hear
what you thought of

#AboutThisBoy
@WalkerBooksUK

@WalkerBooksUK